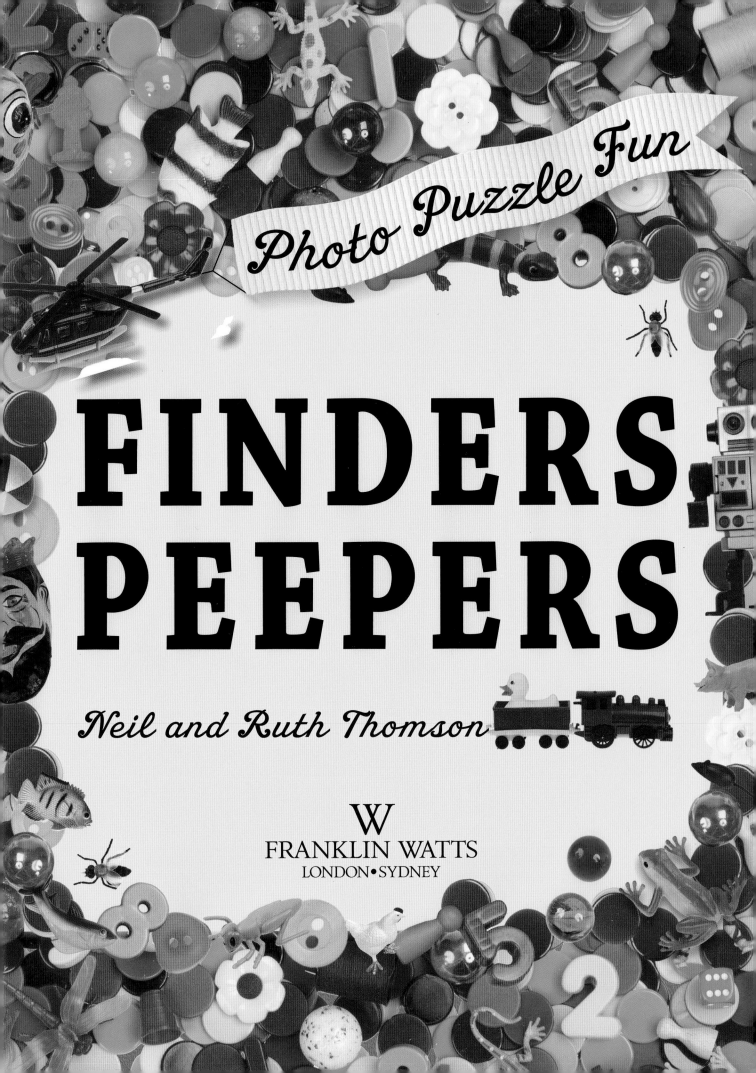

Photo Puzzle Fun

FINDERS PEEPERS

Neil and Ruth Thomson

W

FRANKLIN WATTS
LONDON • SYDNEY

Look, Find and Talk

Welcome to the world of *Finders Peepers* – a book of riches to share and enjoy over and over again. The ten busy themed pictures, crammed with entertaining and colourful details, will encourage young children to look, find and talk.

Simple questions ask children to count, recognise colours, shapes or patterns, or to spot tiny details or differences.

Open questions stimulate the imagination and encourage children to talk at greater length and develop their vocabulary. The book doesn't provide any answers, so you can work them out together.

There are also easy games, including I-spy and matching pairs, as well as activities, such as making animal sounds and movements.

Enjoy asking some of the additional questions on pages 26-27 or doing some of the related activities suggested on pages 28-29.

Have lots of fun using the pictures as a springboard for making up your own stories, games and activities.

Contents

Finders Sweeteners

Find two teddies eating sweets.

5

Which plate has the most cakes?

How old is the birthday bear?

What food would you like at a party?

What present would you give to teddy?

Finders Creepers

How many bugs are caught in the sticky spider's web?

Find an insect with a stripy body and wings.

Count the red ladybirds with blue spots.

8

Which is your favourite creepy crawly?

Count the green grasshoppers.

Can you move like a snake?

Up in the Air

How many red planes are there?

Count the helicopters. What colours are they?

Spot all the planes with propellers.

Which plane do you think is the fastest?

Which planes are decorated with stars?

Which plane would you like to fly?

Finders Squeakers

Spot three mice with curly tails.

Which colour button do you like best?

Find a square button.

Choose a button. Is there a matching one?

What are the mice looking for?

Count the cotton reels.

Animal Allsorts

Spot 1 giraffe, 2 chimpanzees and 3 pigs.

Which animals live on a farm?

I spy an animal with big ears and a trunk. Can you? Now it's your turn.

Which animal would you like as a pet?

Find the squirrels.

Make the noises of the animals.

Toy Cupboard

Find 1 clown, 2 racing cars, 3 ducks, 4 red mice and 5 soft toys.

Find a musical instrument.

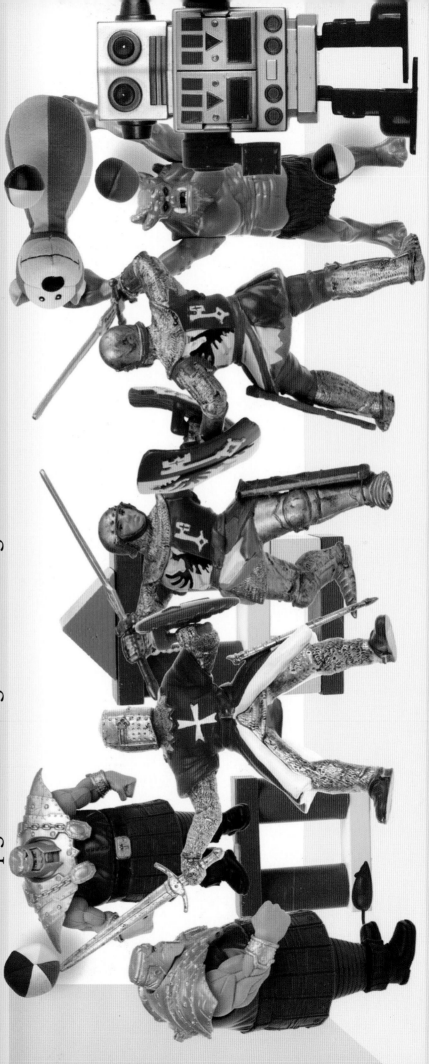

I spy a silver toy with red eyes. What is it? Your turn next.

Why do you think the knights are fighting? Who do you think will win?

17

Very Fishy

Count the seahorses.

How many fish are upside down?

Imagine being a fish. What would it be like?

Find a blue fish swimming from left to right.

Describe your favourite fish.

Find two fish facing one another.

Mask Parade

Which mask would you like to wear?

Which animals have sharp teeth?

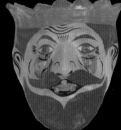
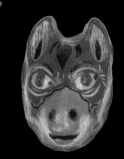

Find an upside-down mask.

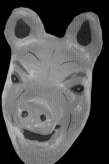

Find matching pairs of masks.

Who looks happy?

Who has the biggest ears?

Traffic Jam

Count the bicycles.

Are there more silver vehicles or red ones?

What has caused this traffic jam?

Spot all the cars with open doors.

Which vehicle do you think is the fastest?

Which vehicle would you like to drive? Where would you go?

What will happen next?

Finders Peepers

Find two dice with matching spots.

Spot the numbers from 1 to 6.

24

Find nine things that appear
on other pages of this book.

More to Find

Look through the book again and do some more talking.

6-7 Finders Sweeteners

- Count the teddy bear's guests (1 rabbit, 4 squirrels and 6 teddies).
- Who is eating a strawberry? Who is wearing a bib? Who is eating a biscuit?
- Play *Spot the cupcake*. 'I spy a cupcake with green icing and four silver balls. Can you? Now it's your turn.'
- Are there more sweets with purple wrappers or with green wrappers?

8-9 Finders Creepers

- Count different kinds of creepy crawlies (flies, red and blue ants, spiders, frogs, lizards and yellow and blue beetles).
- Which creatures are reptiles (snakes and lizards)?
- Find all the creepy crawlies with more than six legs (spiders and centipedes).
- Spot all the creatures with spots.
- What songs and rhymes do you know about creepy crawlies?

10-11 Up in the Air

- Count the biplanes (the planes with two pairs of wings fixed one above the other).
- Which planes carry lots of passengers (look for those with lots of windows)?
- Find the planes made from recycled bits and pieces. Can you see what the makers have used (drinks cans, bottle tops, ring pulls, spark plug, wire)?
- Spot two identical blue planes and three identical red planes.

12-13 Finders Squeakers

- Find all the different-shaped buttons and beads: square, rectangle, hexagon (six-sided), star, oval, flower.
- Describe the difference between two buttons, e.g. one is dark blue and has four holes; the other is pale blue and has two holes.
- Play *Spot the button*. 'I spy a small, round purple button with two holes. Can you find any others that are similar? Now it's your turn.'
- Name the sewing equipment – cotton reels, pins, scissors, tape measure, and thimbles. What's missing? (A needle)

14-15 *Animal Allsorts*

- Spot pairs of tortoises, turkeys and elephants.
- Which animals have stripes?
- Name the animals with hooves (donkey, horse, cow, bull, goat, sheep, deer)?
- Count the dogs.
- Name the birds (cockerel, hen, chick, duck and turkey).

16-17 *The Toy Cupboard*

- Can you find these? Two toys with pink ears. A toy with a red nose; one wearing sunglasses; one with a brown tail; one with blue hands; one with a grey trunk. Three toys waving swords.
- Find things that begin with the same sound: 'p' (pig, princess), 'r' (rabbit, robot), 'c' (car, cat), 'tr' (train, truck, trumpet), 'm' (mouse, monster).
- Count the balls. How many of them have fallen out of the truck?
- Name the objects that rhyme: star/car, truck/duck, plane/train.

18-19 *Very Fishy*

- Choose any fish. Find others exactly the same. Are there more yellow fish with black stripes or red fish with white stripes?
- Use the fish to talk about positions: Find five fish pointing *downwards* and another five pointing *upwards*. Find a red stripy fish swimming from *left* to *right*. Find three pairs of fish *facing* each other. Point to the fish *above* the shark's nose. Find two seahorses *behind* red seaweed.

20-21 *Mask Parade*

- Take turns to describe an animal to spot, e.g. 'I spy a yellow face with spots, black horns and whiskers. Can you?'
- Count how many you can find of each of these masks – ones with moustaches; red eyes; yellow flowers on their heads; whiskers; crowns; black noses.

22-23 *Traffic Jam*

- Find the vehicles that carry goods – tanker, truck, van. What do you think they might be carrying? Where are they going?
- Point to these parts of a car – bonnet, lights, number plate, wing mirrors, wheels and tyres, windscreen, windscreen wipers, bumper, engine, spare tyre, boot, gear stick.
- Find the vehicles made from recycled metal. Can you see what the makers have used (drinks cans, scrap wire)?

24-25 *Finders Peepers*

- Find pairs of dice with matching numbers of spots.
- What number is *above* a red marble? What number is *between* a fish and an insect? What number is *next* to the princess? What number is *above* a dice with four spots?
- Spot two green marbles with orange markings. Spot a white marble with coloured spots. Count the red marbles and the pale blue ones.
- Find a red counter next to a green one. Find a yellow counter under a dark blue one. (The possibilities for this finders peepers game are endless!)

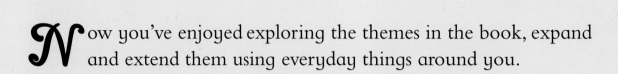

More to Do

Now you've enjoyed exploring the themes in the book, expand and extend them using everyday things around you.

Finders Sweeteners

• Imagine the teddy bears in the picture could talk. What sort of conversations might they be having?

• Have your own teddy bears' picnic indoors or outside. Make some real mini cupcakes and biscuits. Decorate them together.

Finders Creepers

• Look at creepy crawlies' legs, which helps identify them. Snakes have none, lizards have four, insects have six, spiders have eight and centipedes have lots.

• Go for a bug hunt in the garden or a wild patch of ground. Notice where you find them, as this is often a clue about what they eat.

Up in the Air

• Point out the various parts of a plane – cockpit, wings, tail, jet engines or propellers. Talk about what they are for.

• Talk about going on a journey in an aeroplane. What does it feel like to take off and land? What might you see out of the window? Where are you going?

Finders Squeakers

• Spread your own button collection on a table. Add some other small things to find, such as coins, beads, marbles, paperclips, miniature toys, games pieces, etc.

• Talk about how shapes of buttons differ. Why are most buttons round?

• Pick out 10 buttons of varying sizes. Ask children to line them up by size.

Animal Allsorts

- Compare the features of different sorts of animals – fierce ones and tame ones; mammals, birds and reptiles; those that live in hot or cold places; those with hooves or claws; those that climb trees or burrow underground.

- Which animals are the odd ones out (dinosaurs)? Ask why.

The Toy Cupboard

- Imagine the toys in the picture come alive at night. Discuss what they might do.

- Invent conversations between two of the toys in the picture, for example, the ogre and the princess; the robot and the alien; the clown and a knight.

- Hide a toy somewhere in the room and let your child ask questions to help find it.

Very Fishy

- Spot how many different kinds of fish there are in the picture. Look in a book about fish to name them (most are tropical).

- Point out the parts of a fish – fins, tail, scales, gills – and talk about what they are for.

Mask Parade

- Explore why and when people wear masks.

- Make up a story using some of the mask characters. Add animal noises to add drama to your story. Involve the child in choosing which animals to include.

- Make a painted card mask to wear.

Traffic Jam

- When you go for a walk or a car ride, talk about the different sorts of vehicles you see. Why do rescue vehicles have flashing lights and make beeping noises? What loads are carried in tankers, flat-bed trucks and vans? Where are jeeps useful?

- Look at road signs and traffic lights. How do these help prevent traffic jams?

Finders Peepers

- Muddle up different games pieces and help your child sort them out again.

- Play with coloured counters. Make repeating lines, patterns and shapes in contrasting colours. Lay counters out in number rows from one to ten. Use them for adding and taking away.

Franklin Watts
Published in Great Britain in 2017 by The Watts Publishing Group

Text © Ruth Thomson 2014
Photographs © Neil Thomson 2014

Editor: Rachel Cooke
Designer: Sophie Wilkins

The authors and publisher would like to thank Leo Allan, Jane Lee and Finn Carlow for their help with this book. The recycled toys come from the knowtrash collection. See www.knowtrash.com

Dewey Classification: 793.7'3
ISBN: 978 1 4451 2688 3

Printed in China

Franklin Watts
An imprint of
Hachette Children's Group
Part of The Watts Publishing Group
Carmelite House
50 Victoria Embankment
London EC4Y 0DZ

An Hachette UK Company
www.hachette.co.uk

www.franklinwatts.co.uk

MIX
Paper from responsible sources
FSC
www.fsc.org
FSC® C104740